MAPS OF EXETER'S WESTERN ASPECT

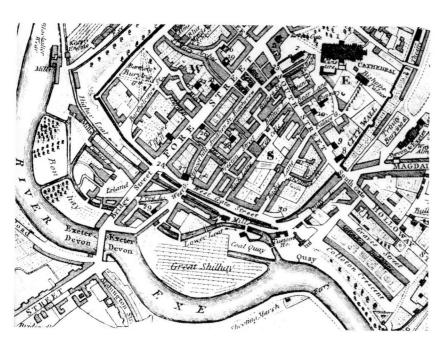

2 – In 1830 it is shown Exeter's West Side had been partially developed on these areas and Shilhay was occupied by racks used for the drying of woollen cloth.

Opposite: 1– A map of 1618 shows extensive areas on the west side of Exeter where the land has been drained and leats cut. Water was used to power mills constructed beside and over the leats. The river was crossed by an arched stone bridge built in 1200.

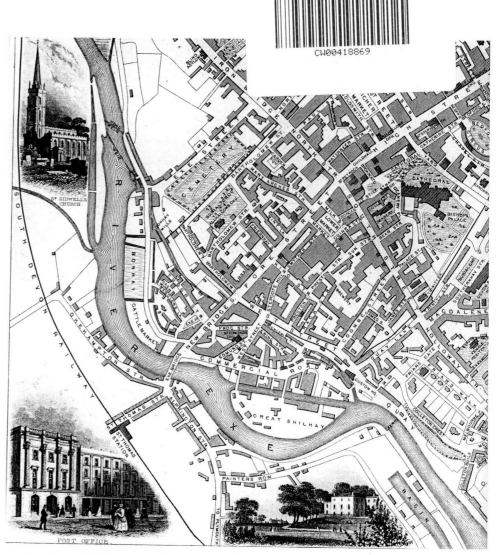

3 – In 1851 Shilhay and Exe Island are shown very developed and the Cattle Market has been created on the edge of the river in Bonhay Road.

1

AERIAL VIEWS OF THE WEST SIDE

5 – Exe Island is shown left with the Cattle Market adjacent to Exe Bridge. Commercial Road is shown right.

Opposite: 4 – This view of the west side of Exeter taken around 1960 shows the extent of development in the riverside areas and the single span steel Exe Bridge opened in 1905.

6 – A view from above Shilhay shows West Street, right, continuing to join Exe Bridge. The area is shown prior to demolition for the construction of Western Way Inner by Pass.

7 – The Quay and Shilhay are recorded with West Street continuing above the city wall, seen right. The leat known as Coney Lake, which divided Shilhay is seen joining the River Exe at the bottom of the photo.

8 – Exeter Quay is shown in its full extent in this record. West Street can be seen behind the Custom House. The density of buildings is particularly noticeable.

THE CHOLERA EPIDEMIC OF 1832

A devastating epidemic of cholera hit the west side of Exeter in 1832 killing many local residents. Poor housing and insanitary conditions helped to fuel the disease. Water taken from the river and leats was a major factor in the spread of cholera.

9 – Water Works were built on the site at Engine Bridge in 1695.

10 – Battery Steps, situated behind the Custom House was a favourite place for drawing water from the leats.

11 – Water was taken from the river by Water Bearers who would sell it in central Exeter for ½d a bucket or three buckets for 1d.

12 – Impoverished conditions in Rack Close Lane helped spread the disease.

13 – Stepcote Hill was the playground for poorer children. An open gutter ran down the medieval street.

14 – As the cholera epidemic took hold barrels of smoking tar were placed in the streets in an attempt to kill the disease.

15 – The dead were taken away in a covered carriage to be disposed of in mass graves. Clothes were burnt and bedding washed in the leats.

16 – The area of Shilhay was used for burning the clothes of victims.

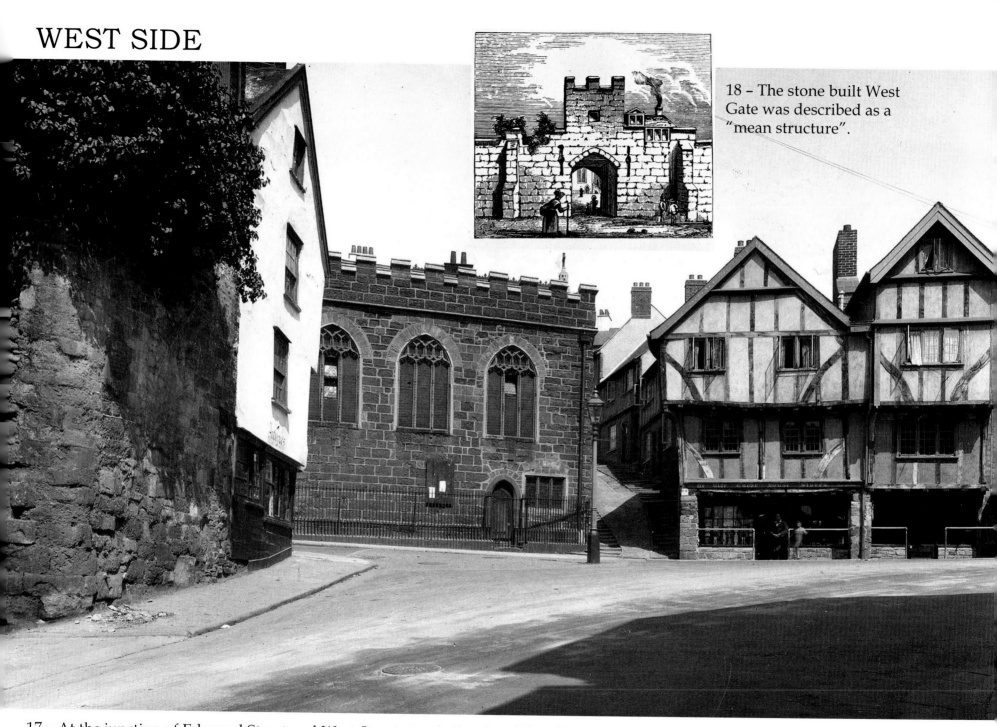

18 – The stone built West Gate was described as a "mean structure".

17 – At the junction of Edmund Street and West Street stands the site of the old West Gate. An ancient timber frame house stood adjacent to the site. St Mary Steps Church, Stepcote Hill and two fine period houses completed a scene that had greeted visitors for centuries

19 – The West Gate site is still marked by a Victorian bronze plaque. The narrow Rack Close Lane is seen left.

20 – The period property shown was removed in the early 1940's, only to be replaced by another period property dating from the early 15th century in 1961.

8

22 – Records of the interior of St Mary Steps Church are relatively scarce but the interior holds an early Norman font.

23 – Passing time outside St Mary Steps Church.

21 – St Mary Steps Church is shown around 1920. The building opposite on the West gate site is shown in a state of disrepair.

24 – West Street looking southwards, showing the line of the city wall. *c* 1910

25 – A detailed record shows washing hanging out of windows to dry and a donkey and cart in West Street.

26 – Timber framed houses dating from the 15th and 16th centuries adjacent to Stepcote Hill. Only the far left properties were to survive.

27 – No 11 Stepcote Hill is shown neglected in this excellent record of circa 1890.

28 – A detailed section of photo 27 shows a water conduit situated at the bottom of Stepcote Hill and at its base a sunken stone bowl providing drinking water for horses. The water supply was piped from Lions Halt to Milk Street down to Stepcote Hill.

29 – No's 11 and 12 West Street were saved and restored in the 1930s.

30-31 – Two rare photos show people gathering in West Street two days after the death of Queen Victoria. An open barouche with dignitaries is flanked by militia on horse back. Date 24th January 1901

32 – Gathering around a street vendor.

33 – Daily street scene in West Street. Circa 1910.

34 – Donkey and cart in West Street.

35 – Street vendor.

36 – A horse drawn dust cart is recorded in West Street whilst children crowd around a covered wagon.
An early motorbike is also shown. *c* 1920.

37 – Detail of horse drawn dust cart.

Opposite: 39 – West Street, seen truncated circa 1961, shows Cricklepit Mill and Leat Terrace behind.

38 – West Street at the junction with Quay Hill. Properties were removed in the 1960s.

40 – The construction of Western Way inner by pass
eliminated much of the west side of Exeter.

41 – Follets Buildings, a tenement block overlooking
Coombe Street, was home for a number of poorer families.
Western Way construction is shown in its last stages.

THE 1930s SLUM CLEARANCE

A rare series of photos taken before the slum clearance in the early 1930s records the state of properties and area around Stepcote Hill.

42 – The junction with Preston Street and West Street shows a covered cart belonging to the Cathedral Dairy, selling products.

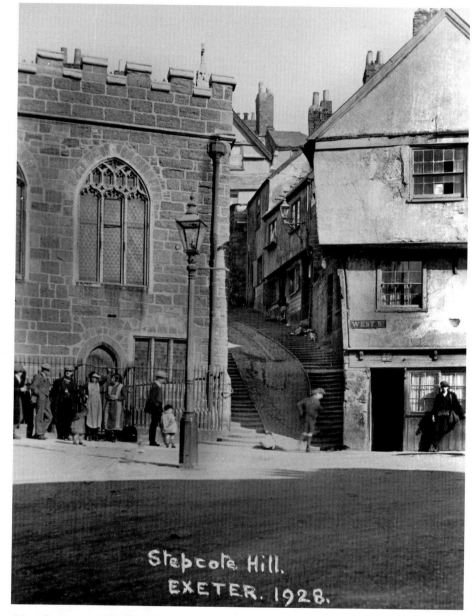

44 – Stepcote Hill 1928.

45 – West Street and Stepcote Hill showing dilapidated houses.

Opposite: 43 – West Street looking south. To the left is Pearse & Co, specialists in bones, skin, hair and metal recycling. The company also had premises on Shilhay. No 15/16 is the Exeter Tyre Rerubbering Works.

46 – No 11 West Street in poor condition.

47 – View looking down Stepcote Hill to no 11 West Street. Ancient timbers have been rendered over.

Stepcote Hill
EXETER
1928.

48 – The centre of Stepcote Hill 1928.

49 – A view down Preston Street showing original warehouses with handcarts outside.

50 – Upper Stepcote Hill north side 1928.

51 – Upper Stepcote Hill
with City Arms Inn.

51a – Detail of City Arms Inn.

52 – Washing hanging in a backyard.

53 – Rear of properties.

54 – The courtyard Georges Court.

55 – View to Stepcote hill from the junction with Smythen Street.

Opposite: 56 – Fish and Chip Saloon on the corner of Stepcote Hill and King Street.

57 – View down King Street from junction with Stepcote Hill.

Preston Street from West Street showing lorries advertising W Brock & Co Furnishers.

59 – West Street after the removal of corner building at West Gate site. *c* 1942.

60 – Demolition at Stepcote Hill 1930s.

61 – View up Stepcote Hill *c* 1910.

62 – A local family recorded in Parsonage Alley off Stepcote Hill *c* 1900.

THE FAMOUS MEDIEVAL STEPCOTE HILL

Ancient thoroughfare into Exeter from the west.

63 – No 11 West Street at the start of Stepcote Hill from West Street.

64 – An open gutter runs down Stepcote Hill.

65 – Houses on Stepcote Hill are decorated with window boxes.

66 – Making her way home.

STEPCOTE HILL EXETER 10600

68 – Improvements have been made to the central gutter but properties are shown without their roof tiles.

67 – Derelict property in Stepcote Hill.

35

69 – A fine record of Stepcote Hill. A sign
states "House to Let "at the top of the hill.

70 – The childrens'
playground.

71 – In this record properties are shown in a good state of repair. Stepcote Hill Sunday School is shown left.

PRESTON STREET

73 – Preston Street (the street of the priests) was noted for some fine timber framed buildings as is shown in this exceptional record dating from around 1890. It was taken by Mr Tremlett, a tannery owner and photographer.

74 – At the turn of the 20th century Preston Street still retained a number of interesting period buildings. The pair of gabled properties shown were demolished for slum clearance. Circa 1920.

Opposite: 72 – A wonderful record of old Preston Street shows typical shops and dwellings in one of Exeter's back streets.

75 – Situated at the east end of Preston Street the local pub, The Sawyers Arms, took its name from an ancient trade – Sawyer being a man who cuts timber for a living. It was a popular community pub but removed in the 1970s Photo c 1960.

76 – A little girl rides the bakers horse in Preston Street.

78 – Taken around 1965 this photograph records the properties occupied by Fred Ford Signs.
The buildings incorporate the last remains of the structure of an early timber frame building that was later demolished.

77 – Looking from Preston Street eastwards to the Cathedral. *c* 1960.

79 – A rare image shows Feys Dining Rooms in Guinea Street on the corner of Milk Street and next to the Lower Market. Photo *c* 1920.

CENTRAL SCHOOL, RACK STREET

80 – Central School was often referred to as Rack Street Naval College. The origin of this expression was shrouded in mystery but with the help of its former teachers it was discovered that in its early years the late Victorian School had taught maritime navigation giving a connection to the city's maritime trading. The school, a focal point of the West Quarter community was demolished in 1979.

Opposite: 83 – Children at Central School pose for the Exeter photographer Henry Wykes in July 1945.

81 – Central School staff *c* 1890.

82 – School classroom.

84 – Central School staff *c* 1958.
Bottom left: Mrs G Hill, Miss Nancy Daw, Mrs Bowden
Head Mistress: Miss Turner.
Top left: Mr Strickland, Mr Hodge.

85 – Playground activities

86, 87, 88, 89

Children in the playground.

92 – An early drawing indicates the style of shops found in Smythen Street.

91 – Smythen Street , an early reference to blacksmiths, was also named Butchers Row that at one time lined the street with open fronted shops.

Opposite: 90 – Demolition of Central School 1979.

93 – The junction of Smythen Street and King Street still displays the style of earlier buildings in this record of 1949. F W J Pike operated a Fish and Chip Salon that may have taken the place of the Salon demolished on the opposite side of the street in the 1930s.

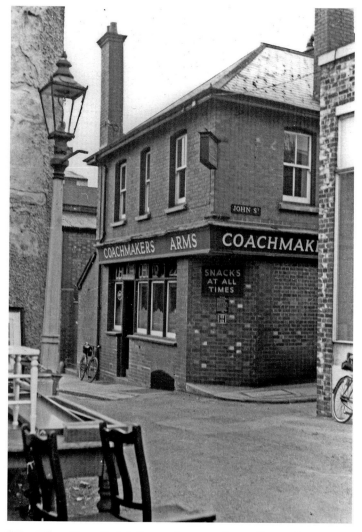

95 – The Coach Makers Arms after alterations to the façade and front door. *c* 1960.

94 – A rare view of John Street is shown from Smythen Street with older buildings still lining the narrow thoroughfare. With removal of the main structure of St John's Church in 1937 only the tower was left standing. The building next to the Coach Makers Arms was integrated into the pub.

96, 97, 98
Evans Gadd Wholesale Druggists and Stationers had occupied premises in Fore Street at the turn of the 20th century but were to acquire land in Smythen Street. The company built an impressive and unique Art Deco building of substantial proportions on the site but despite protests it was demolished in the 1990s.

99 – A charming drawing by George Townsend gave a nostalgic view of old King Street.

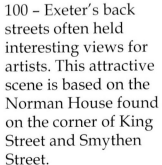

100 – Exeter's back streets often held interesting views for artists. This attractive scene is based on the Norman House found on the corner of King Street and Smythen Street.

101 – The building known as the Norman House was identified by a decorated Norman arch over the door. The building is shown partly derelict. It was, however, restored and became a small museum only to be bombed in May 1942.

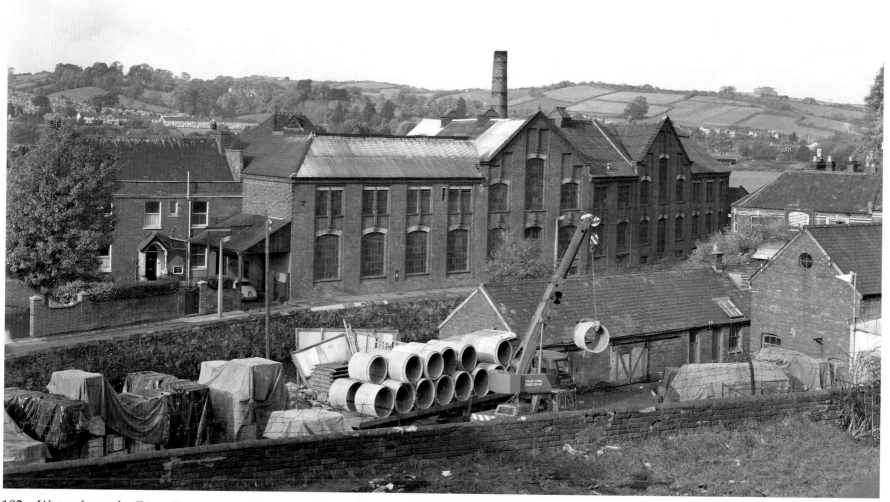

102 – Water from the River Exe was used to create leats to power local mills. A large mill on the site at Engine Bridge known as Head Weir Mill produced paper and today is called The Mill on the Exe. Previous mills on the site were used for fulling, and corn milling.

103 – Two leats were to flow from Engine Bridge – the Higher and Lower Leats. The open Lower Leat is shown running beside Bonhay Road. It is now culverted.

104 – The Higher Leat still flows at the rear of Tudor Street and passes under New Bridge Street.

105 – Cleaning of the leats was an annual event with prisoners sometimes being used for the purpose.

106 – The Higher Leat running towards the Quay can still be seen at New Bridge Street seen here in the late 1970s.

107 – This unique scene records the Lower Leat forming a shallow lake at the rear of the City Brewery in Commercial Road. The leat continued flowing under the ancient medieval bridge towards the Quay.

108 – The Higher Leat was constructed to run beside the city wall and Cricklepit Lane. The water flow was used to power Cricklepit Mill. Workers cottages overlooked the leat at this point.

109 – Leat Terrace.

110 – Leat Terrace, a small row of early cottage was demolished in the 1970s.

111 – Water from the Higher Leat was used in the tanning process at Tremletts Tannery shown at the end of the Higher Leat at Cricklepit. *c* 1910.

113 – A subsidiary waterwheel operated in the Higher Leat, below Cricklepit Mill, during the early 20th century but eventually became derelict.

112 – Internal waterwheel at Cricklepit Mill. *c* 1987.

114 – Bridge over the Higher Leat at New Mill.

115 – Aerial view of Shilhay before removal of buildings. Photo 1960.

116 – Detail of Shilhay 1960.

114 – Oblique aerial view of the River Exe and Shilhay from the northwest.

115 – An early drawing of Shilhay depicts timber drying sheds, circa 1850.

119 – Dwellings constructed on the medieval Exe Bridge over sailed the
River Exe and gave access to water by the use of dipping steps.

Pages 66-67: 120 –One of the finest engravings
of Exeter shows the City from the west and
depicts Shilhay as a large open area used for
the drying of woollen cloth. Date 1810.

121 – Commercial Road is seen from the Junction with Edmund Street. To the far left is Tremletts Tannery. Underneath the road and beside the Tannery ran the Lower Leat. In earlier times this site was referred to as Horse Pool. Photo *c* 1930.

122 – A substantial building overlooked the river from Commercial Road occupied by Gilchrist and Fisher, makes of Kingfisher bags. The entry to Coney Lake is seen right flowing beside the factory of J L Thomas & Co. *c* 1960.

123 – View from Commercial Road towards Exe Bridge.

124 – A drawing by Miss Primrose Pitman shows the gas works as seen from New Bridge Street. In the foreground are the remains of the medieval bridge dating from 1200 that was uncovered in the early 1970s.

125 – The north end of Commercial Road was partly lined with workers cottages.

126 – Cottages in Commercial Road had toilets extending over the Lower Leat.

124 – A number of warehouses operated from Commercial Road near the Bishop Blaize Pub. This included part of Tremletts Tannery.

128 – Interior of Tremletts Tannery.

129 – The Northam Foundry had operated from Commercial Road and was recorded as early as 1825. It was one of a number of foundries in Exeter.

130 – A rare coloured drawing depicts a fine mill on Shilhay which may be Cricklepit Mill. However there is some uncertainty.

131 – The Lower Leat ran down Commercial Road on the east side and could be seen uncovered near the Bishop Blaize Pub where it was walled and railed as shown in this drawing.

132 – The Bishop Blaize pub is Exeter's oldest public house outside the city wall and was named after Bishop Blaize who was martyred after having his skin flailed off by the use of Wool combs.

133 – A small stone pedestrian footbridge crossed the leat at the Bishop Blaize Pub. Circa 1960.

The Bridge at Cricklepit Mills near West Gate

Exeter Pub.d Sep.l 1834 at J Gendall's St Peter's Church Yard.

134 – An etching dated 1834 by John Gendall shows a footbridge at Cricklepit Mill.

135 – Cricklepit Mill is shown occupied by W G Shears Miller and Corn Merchant. Circa 1988.

136 – An aerial view of Shilhay showing Victoria Playground adjacent to Bodleys Foundry,
an unusual site for a playground. West Street and the city wall are seen right.

137 – A view from West Street over looking Shilhay shows Bodleys Foundry and the drying shed adjacent to Cricklepit Mill. Photo 1960.

138 – A view over the Quay circa 1965 from Horse Lane shows the Transit Shed, Public Toilets and Weigh Bridge used by HM Customs and Excise.

138 – Advert for night clubs. Disused warehouses were refurbished to become Exeter's night spot from the 1960s onwards.

140 – Aerial view of the Quay from the south looking north.

142 – Steel piles driven into the rivers edge and concreted tamed the River Exe as it flowed past Exeter.

141 – Clearance of Shilhay in the 1970s.

143 – Major riverside changes was to avoid major flooding in later years. View to Exe Bridge.

COOMBE STREET
&
JAMES STREET

Coombe Street gives access to South Street from West Street.

144 – Coombe Street, as seen from Quay Hill. The street allowed an easier alternative to the steepness of Fore Street and Stepcote Hill.

145 – An early record shows a decorative arch extending across Coombe Street to mark an agricultural event. It states *"God save the plough"*. Circa 1900.

146 – Dilapidated properties are shown at the top of Quay Hill. Late 1930s.

148 – The staff at Raddans Printing Works.

147 – The local printing company Raddans Printing Works are shown celebrating Coronation day in 1953.

149 – Coombe Street celebrates Coronation Day outside the The Duke of York pub and Raddans Printing Works.

150 –The yard at the rear of the White Hart Hotel South Street is shown with the entrance in Coombe Street. A covered wagon is parked in the yard and a sign indicates "Animal Dispensary". The small warehouse is occupied by J Berry & Sons Wool Stores and also selected seeds.

151 – James Street ran from Coombe Street to South Street and was abutting the city wall.

152 – A row of fine period properties flanked the west side of the street but were to fall into disrepair.

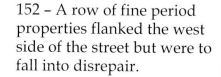

153 – A rare painting by the Exeter artist John Shapland depicts local women at work in the wash house.

154 – This view recorded from Central School looks westward towards the Haldon Hills. The large central building was the Public Bath House, a facility used by many local people in the West Quarter. It was demolished in the early 1970s.

THE QUAY

The creation of a Quay at Exeter brought wealth to the city. Many local people in the West Quarter benefited from the importing and exporting of products from the Quay.

155 – An artist's impression of the Quay in the 16th century W Cotton Printed 1873.

EXETER QVAY,
IN THE 16TH CENTVRY.

W. Cotton. delt.

Frank Walker. litho.

156 – Quay Bridge by F C Lewis 1827.

Etchd. & Pubd. by F.C.Lewis, 1827.

157 – The leats from Quay Bridge 1827.

158 – An early drawing of Quay Bridge and the Custom House showing a fenced area (left) for the storage of coal.

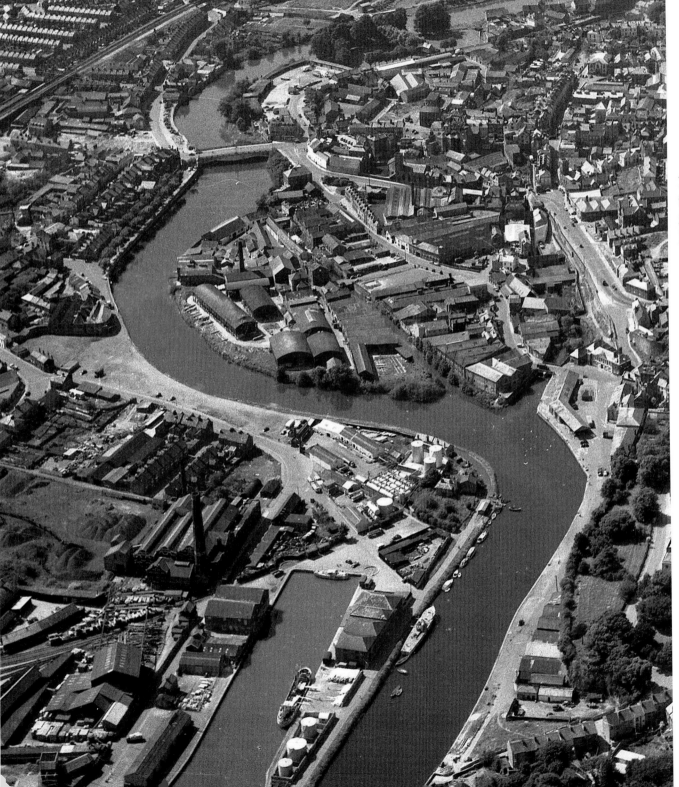

159 – An aerial view of the Quay and Shilhay from the south. Circa late 1950s.

160 – The Custom House and Quay c 1950. The buildings in the background no longer exist.

162 – An image from
a lantern slide records
masted ships at the
Quay. *c* 1890.

161 – A fine record of the Quay shows the transit
shed surrounded by travelling wagons. The
Prospect Inn is named The Fountain Inn.

163 – A fine day on the Quay looking towards Shilhay.

164 – Ship offloading at the Quay circa 1910.

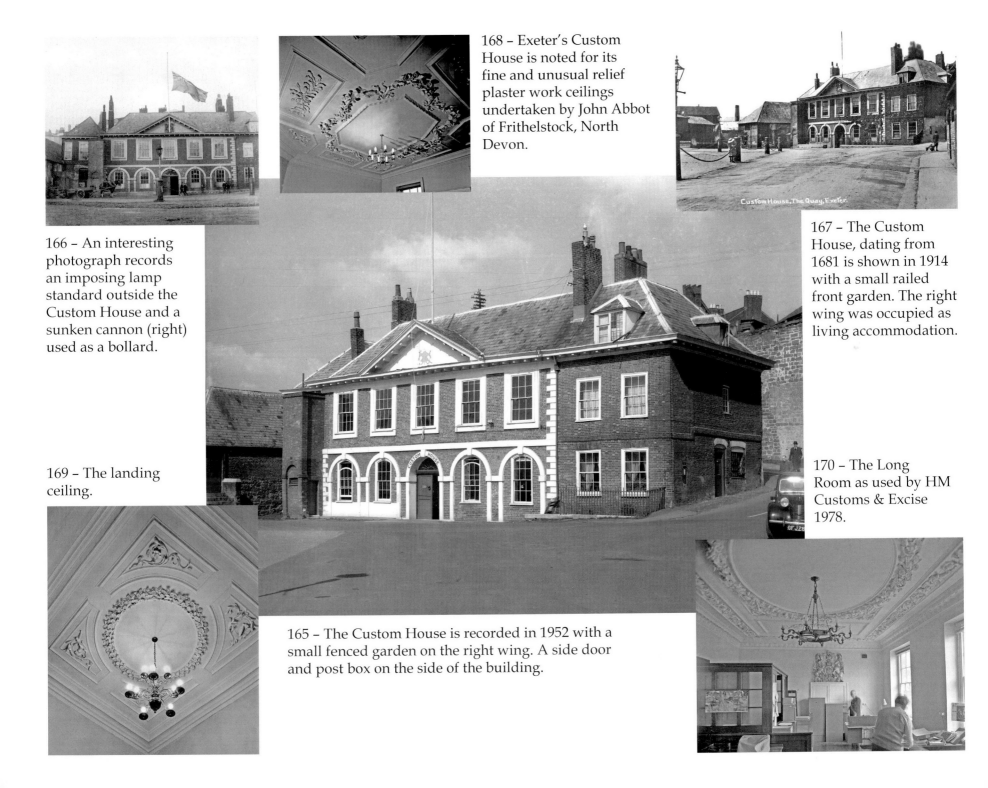

168 – Exeter's Custom House is noted for its fine and unusual relief plaster work ceilings undertaken by John Abbot of Frithelstock, North Devon.

166 – An interesting photograph records an imposing lamp standard outside the Custom House and a sunken cannon (right) used as a bollard.

167 – The Custom House, dating from 1681 is shown in 1914 with a small railed front garden. The right wing was occupied as living accommodation.

169 – The landing ceiling.

170 – The Long Room as used by HM Customs & Excise 1978.

165 – The Custom House is recorded in 1952 with a small fenced garden on the right wing. A side door and post box on the side of the building.

171 – The Wharfingers Office (a Manager for the Quay) is shown in 1978 as the offices of The International Sailing Craft Association. The adjacent premises, a DIY store, was later discovered to be the intact Elizabethan transit shed and dock.

173 – A view taken in 1927 from the top of the city wall to Horse Lane records the collapsed section.

172 – In 1927 the City Wall at the junction of Quay Hill and Quay Lane collapsed on to The Custom House Inn that stood at the junction. The damage was so great the remains of the pub were demolished.

174 – The Custom House Inn took its name from the famous building opposite.

175 – The landlord and his family are recorded outside the Custom House Inn.

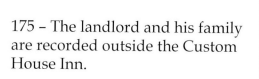

176 – Quay Lane was a direct route from South Street to the Quay. The little hill was lined with small cottages whose gardens extended to the city wall on the north side.

177 – Exeter Quay recreated. This record of Exeter Quay was taken during the filming of the BBC series the Onedin Line that ran from 1971 to 1980.

180 – Exeter Quay is shown in the 1890s from Haven Banks. Horses are pulling stone laden carts up the Quay. Circa 1890.

Opposite: 178 – A rare image records the hand operated ferry crossing the River Exe and the Quay is seen piled with stone waiting to be transported by horse and cart to the city centre.

(*inset*) 179 – Traditionally a ferry service has operated from Exeter Quay since 1614. The original ferry mans cottage stood on the Quay opposite Haven Banks. The painting is by George Townsend circa 1830.

181 – A masted vessel is moored beside the warehouses on the Quay. At this time a small gated yard existed between both buildings.

182 – The River Exe has historically been recognised for its salmon. This record shows John Archibald Lucas, Architect with his Gillie at Exeter Quay with a fine catch in the 1930s.

183 – Exeter Quay and cellars. Circa 1950.

184 – Colleton Cresent and St Leonard's Quay. Circa 1890.

185 – Ships moored at St Leonard's Quay to take on ballast. Circa 1895.

Below left: 186 –View of Exeter Quay from the south showing cannons used as bollards.

Below right: 187 – Scrap iron on St Leonard's Quay. Circa 1900.

188 – Mitchells Monumental Marble, Slate & Stone Works at Haven Banks. Circa 1910.

189 – Interior of Mitchells Works showing bath and fire surrounds.

190 – Drive-in courtyard at Mitchells, Haven Banks.

191 – Mitchells showroom.

192 – The office at Mitchells.

Opposite:
193 – Chimney pots in the yard at Mitchells showing Quay warehouses in the background.

Exeter Corporation Electricity Station.

194 – The Exeter Corporation Electricity Station, opened in 1903, provided electricity for Exeter's new electric trams in 1905. The station chimney was a landmark.

195 – A branch railway line connected to the basin allowed railway trucks to be loaded directly from vessels.

196 – Opened in 1830 the Basin, constructed at the head of the Exeter Ship Canal, gave greater access to vessels offloading at Exeter.

198 – Entry to the Basin from the Canal circa 1910.

197 – Ship at the Basin. Circa 1900.

199 – Reproduced from a lantern slide a busy
scene is captured at Kings Arms Sluice.

200 – Ships facing towards the city at
Kings Arms Sluice.

201 – Timber is shown deposited on both sides of the Basin.

202 – The Lock Keepers cottage at Kings Arms Sluice was demolished by accident in the 20th century.

203 – A rare record shows the Canal virtually drained at Salmon Pool. Date unknown.

204 – For vessels using the Exeter Ship Canal it was necessary to be towed by horse.

205 – One of the last commercial vessels to use the Exeter Ship Canal was the ship Tillerman seen here at Countess Wear Swing Bridge.

206 – Situated just beyond Countess Wear on the Exeter Ship Canal, the site known as The Lime Kilns was at one time inhabited. A stone cottage stood adjacent to the lime kilns. These are the only known records of the cottage.

207 – Lime was transported on the Exeter Ship Canal and deposited at a number of kilns but today this site shows virtually no sign of the previous buildings.

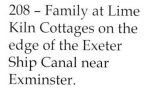

208 – Family at Lime Kiln Cottages on the edge of the Exeter Ship Canal near Exminster.

209 – Edmund Street, taking its name from the church, joined Commercial Road shortly after leaving Exe Bridge on the south side. The junction is recorded from properties abutting Exe Bridge. The public toilets are seen on the edge of the river opposite the City Brewery, right.

EDMUND STREET

The foundations of this street were the remains of the ancient medieval stone bridge built in 1200 to cross the River Exe. With the demolition of the bridge, part of the structure was still retained as a highway but was widened to allow a greater flow of traffic.

210 – A detail from the previous image shows Taylor & Bodley Founders & Engineers who were operating from the old Northam Foundry in Commercial Road.

211 – The tradition of carnivals in Exeter involved a route through the city with tableaux pulled by horses. The carnival is recorded in Edmund Street in 1902.

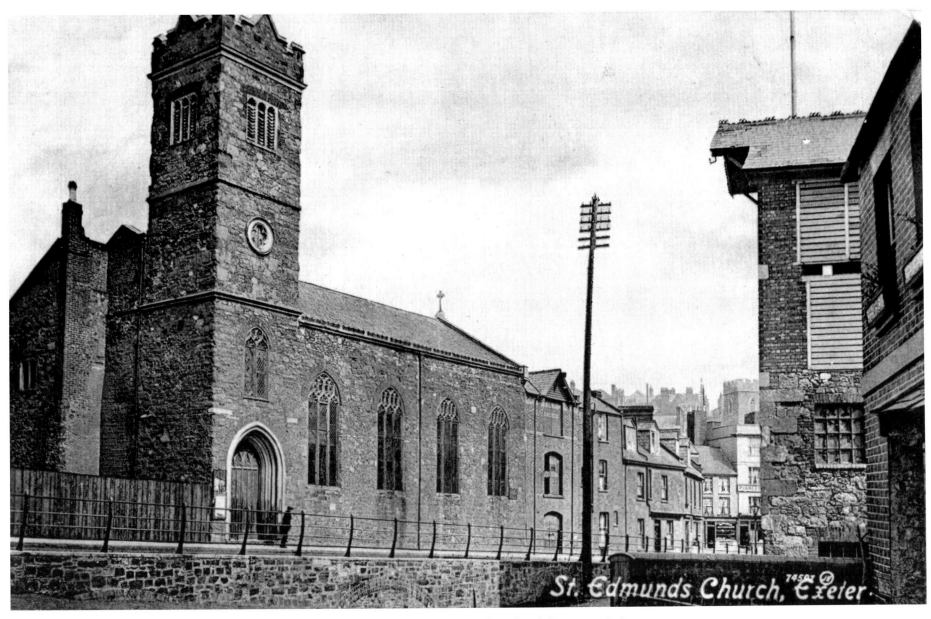

St. Edmunds Church, Exeter.

212 – St Edmunds Church, built beside the ancient medieval Exe Bridge, had Saxon origins.
The church in Edmund Street stood opposite Tremletts Tannery.

214 – Interior of St Edmunds Church.

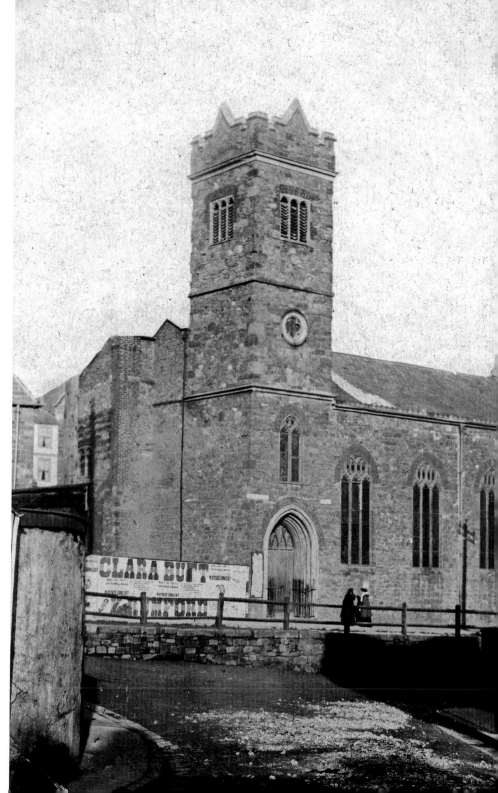

213 – A view from Horse pool to St Edmunds Church.

215 – The Parish Room of St Edmunds Church was situated in a small street on Shilhay.

216 – At the junction of Edmund Street and Frog Street stood one of Exeter's oldest buildings, a timber framed house dating from the early 15th century.

217 – In the 1970's Tremletts Tannery was demolished.

218 – Iron railings marked the end of the medieval Exe Bridge that still formed the foundations of Edmund Street.

219 – Stepcote Hill as seen from the Teignmouth Inn.

220 – The Teignmouth Inn, a pseudo timber framed building, stood on the corner of Ewings Lane.

222 – At the junction with West Street and Edmund Street, Cricklepit Lane led down to Cricklepit Mill and the Higher Leat.

221 – Ewings Lane, entered from Edmund Street, was named after an early landowner. It led to Ewings Square behind the Bishop Blaize pub.

THE FARTHING BREAKFAST

223 – Missionary work was carried out in the West Quarter organised through The Mission Hall on Exe Island. Farthing Breakfasts were distributed in Cricklepit Lane.

224 – A large group of children queque for a Farthing Breakfast looked over by two possible benefactors in this interesting record.

225 – With the construction of Western Way in the 1970s West Street and Edmund Street were radically changed.

226 – St Edmunds Church was not to survive with only its tower left to mark its presence.

THE HOUSE THAT MOVED

A centuries old property was to stand in the way of major road construction, after ten years of debate the decision was made to physically move the building.

227 – No 16 Edmund Street had stood on the corner of Frog Street for five centuries creating a picturesque corner.

228 – Dating from around 1430 the corner property at Edmund Street was a favourite with artists and photographers.

229 – By the turn of the 20th century number 16 Edmund Street was in a dilapidated state. The ground floor had been a traditional open fronted shop with families living above.

230 – In the 1930's some restoration took place and a quatrefoil side window was uncovered.

231 – The Frog Street junction in 1955.

232 – The timber framing of 16 Edmund Street was clearly exposed in the 1950s.

233 – View from Frog Street showing the Teignmouth Inn.

234 – Standing in the way of the construction of Western Way it was proposed to demolish the period building. It was, however saved by a preservation order imposed by the government.

235 – After a ten year disagreement about its future it was decided to remove the building to another site. In 1961 incarcerated in a wooden corset the building was lifted from its original position in December.

236 – Propped and supported No 16 Edmund Street was to move approximately 100 yards up the hill.

237 – Crowds gathered in December 1961 for the moving of the house.

238 – The early dwelling was moved out into Edmund Street.

239 – Iron wheels were fitted to the massive wooden frame.

240 – Iron rails laid in front of the building
allowed it to be winched up the street.

241 – On the move!

242 – Inspecting the ancient timbers that had lasted 500 years.

243 – The removal of the building from the corner of Frog Street would give the opportunity to start demolition.

135

245 – A tight squeeze at the Teignmouth Inn required the necessity for some of the timber cladding to be sawn off.

Opposite: 244 – The property was to be moved in stages. It is shown standing in Edmund Street.

246 – Laying rails in Edmund Street.

247 – The building was placed in position for moving up Edmund Street.

Opposite: 248 – At the junction with Ewings Lane.

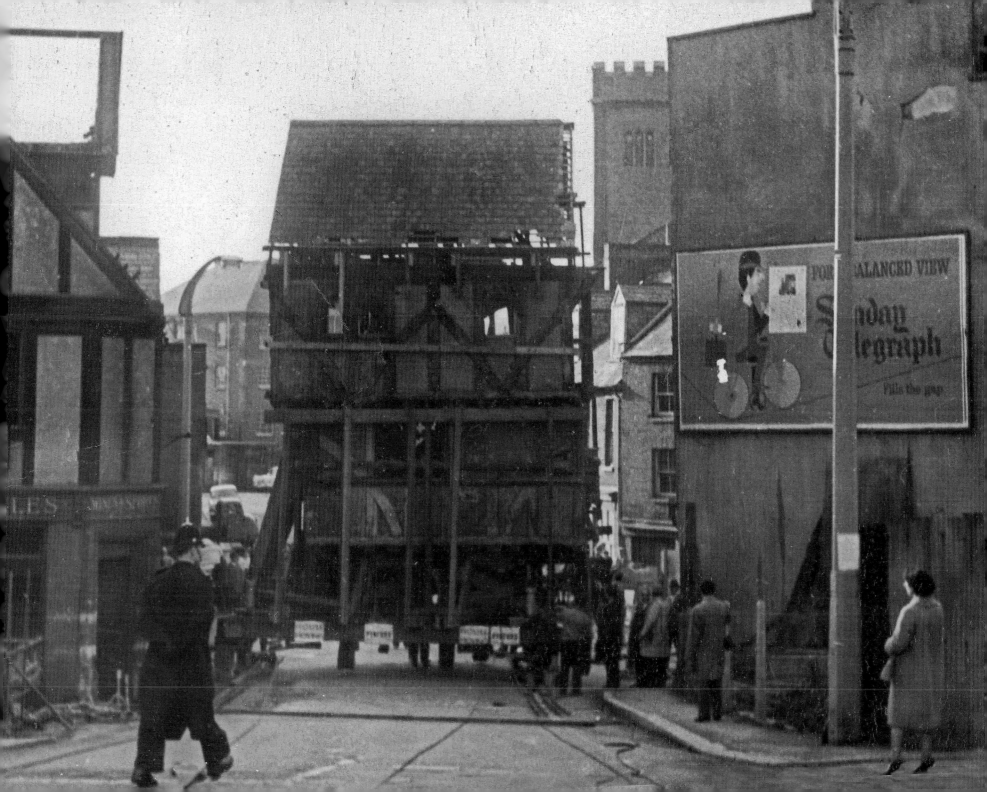

250 – At West Street.

249 – At Ewings Lane.

251 – Readjusting rails at West Street.

252 – House in readiness for the move into the new site at West Gate.

253 – Last adjustments are made before re-siting the house.

255 – Crowds gather at West Street for the reinstatement.

254 – Winching operations in West Street.

Opposite: 256 – Final stages at West Street.

257 –
Foundations
at West Street.

259 – Beginning of restoration.

258 – A new concrete base was prepared for the re-siting of number 16 Edmund Street.

260 – House nearing
completion of restoration.

261 – The restored
property was to become
known as The House
That Moved.

FROG STREET

The ancient street, named after a marshland animal, had existed since the earliest times but was to be swept away as the west side of the city was developed in the 1970's.

262 – Frog Street was a shortcut to Exe Island from Edmund Street.

FROG STREET, (WEST QUARTER).

263 – Frog Street, one of Exeter's oldest thoroughfares, related to the fact that this side of the city was once extensive marshland. A late 19th century drawing shows a small street lined with open fronted shops visited by merchants.

264 – Prior to demolition Frog Street still retained early period properties including Chanters the Bakers.

265 – At the junction with Edmund Street was The Pioneer Coffee Tavern and Lecture Room.

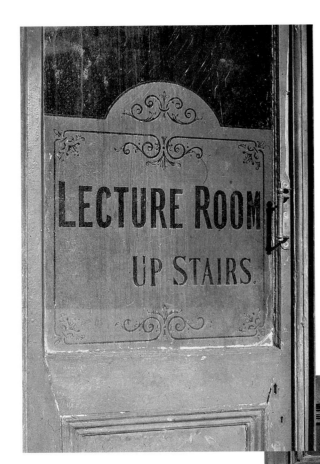

267 – The etched glass door of The Pioneer Coffee Tavern.

268 – The painted window of the tavern depicting The West Gate.

266 – The painted and gilded window of the Pioneer Coffee Tavern stated *"Hot dinners daily from 12pm – 3pm Chips, steak& soups. Tea ,coffee, cocoa and all kinds of summer and winter drinks"*

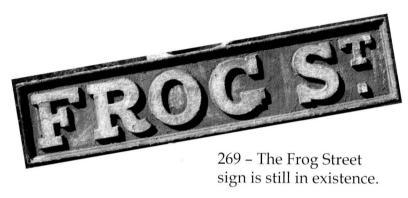

269 – The Frog Street
sign is still in existence.

270 – Central Frog Street looking south.

271 – Beales Garage in Frog Street specialised in Jaguar cars.

272 – At the north end of Frog Street stood the City Brewery stores and the archway leading into Exe Island.

273 – At the north end of Frog Street stood a simple timber framed building possibly dating from the early 15ᵗʰ century. It was however demolished.

274 – View from Frog Street showing the New Bridge Street viaduct.

275, 276 – A series of photos taken from New Bridge Street shows the demolition of Edmund Street and Frog Street.

277 – Demolition of Edmund Street.

278 – Demolition of Beales Garage, Frog Street.

279 – Demolition of Frog Street buildings by bulldozer.

280 – Demolition of Frog Street.

281 – Demolition of Frog Street.

282 – Demolition of Frog Street.

283 – The stone archway connecting Exe Island was to be removed for a new modern concrete bridge.

284 – View looking south after the removal of Beales Garage, Frog Street.

286 – The creation of Western Way obliterated much of the western side of ancient Exeter.

285 – Redevelopment of Frog Street.

Opposite: 287 – Aerial view of
Exe Island & Exe Bridge, *c* 1960.

288 – Detail of Exe Island showing a compact community.

289 – The Exe Island entrance
sign displayed on the archway
to Exe Island circa 1960.

290 – A large slate
sided property stood
next to Exe Island
entrance but was
removed to allow
the continuation
of Western Way
construction.

291 – An informal square formed the centre of Exe Island, of which the east side was a row of Mission Hall buildings.

292 – The Ewings Lane and Exe Island Mission Headquarters at Exe Island consisted of some fine buildings with an entrance leading to the Mission Hall.

293 – The Missionary buildings were to fall into disrepair and partially removed.

294 – The centre of Exe Island before removal of the Mission Hall buildings.

295 – The centre of Exe Island was dominated by a large Heavitree stone building resembling a warehouse. It became the Exe Island Lodging House for men.

296 – The Exe Island Lodging House
side view.

297 – Within Exe Island, opposite
Rosemary Lane and the City
Council Yard, stood a small
Victorian school of which this is
the only known record. The school
was latterly the Central Technical
School Annexe.

299 – The Queen Victoria pub. Circa 1960.

298 – A view looking up Tudor Street from the
Queen Victoria Pub. Circa 1960.

301 – Tudor Street was known for its historic property referred to as "The Tudor House". Its distinctive feature was the scalloped slate decorative front.

300 – An etching by artist Miss Francis Hayman shows work being carried out at Tudor Street.

302 – Tudor Street is shown with gardens opposite the Tudor House. Circa 1910.

303 – No 1 Tudor Street was a tenanted property being occupied by a labourer in 1947 however this record dates from 1897.

304 – The 17th century Tudor House, shown dilapidated, is renowned for its slate frontage incorporating Coats of Arms that relate to its early owners. Circa 1920.

306 – Local Exe Island children.

305 – Children outside the
Tudor House, Exe Island.

307 – Central Tudor Street looking south shows other period properties.

308 – Tudor Street looking north. Circa 1930.

309 – St Edmunds Square. A small group
of cottages with gardens stood at the
north end of Tudor Street. They were
demolished in the 1970s.

310 – The entry from Bonhay Road into
Tudor Street with period properties.
An etching by the artist Miss Francis
Hayman. Circa 1920.

311 – A delightful group of cottages existed on Exe Island adjacent to Parkins Foundry.

313 – An early drawing of Engine Bridge at the junction with Exe Street.

314 – Engine Bridge takes its name from a water engine constructed to pump water up into the city in 1695. Circa 1930.

Opposite: 312 – Properties overlooking the Lower Leat on Exe Island next to Parkins Foundry. Circa 1910.

316 – Pupils at Paradise School. Circa 1910.

315 – Demolition of the north end of Tudor Street showing Paradise School in Bartholomew Terrace. Circa 1978.

317 – Paradise School exercises.

THE CATTLE MARKET, BONHAY ROAD

The Cattle Market at Bonhay Road, built in the mid 19th century, removed the problem of cattle being driven into Exeter's streets where they were sold. The Bonhay Road market was replaced by a new market on Marsh Barton in November 1939 and today operates from a new site at Matford.

319 – A 19th century engraving shows cattle coming to the new Cattle Market in Bonhay Road.

320 – Shepherds regularly drove their sheep down Bonhay Road. Powhay Mill is shown in the background. Circa 1910.

318 – Exeter's first purpose built Cattle Market was built on the edge of the River Exe in Bonhay Road just beyond Exe Bridge. It provided a convenient site for cattle drovers and shepherds without having to come into the city centre.

321 – A rare record of the Cattle Market. Circa 1900.

322 – Men and cattle.

323 – Eyeing up the stock.

324 – Cattle sale.

325 – Good beasts.

326 – Stall at the Cattle Market.

327 – Prime show cattle at the Devon County Show.

To Millers, Corn Factors,
Contractors, and Others.

TO BE SOLD

BY AUCTION,

BY HUSSEY AND SON,

On FRIDAY, the 6th day of JUNE next, at 11 o'clock in the
Forenoon, in the CATTLE MARKET, Exeter,

FOUR CAPITAL DRAUGHT

HORSES

IN EXCELLENT CONDITION,

With 7 sets of handsome brass-mounted cart-horse Harness,
nearly new; also 2 very substantial well-built covered

WAGGONS,

On springs, one of which is fitted with Collings' Patent Axles, and
equal to three tons' weight.

The above is the property of the Okehampton Flour and Coal Company, and will be
Sold in consequence of a dissolution of their partnership.

Also 3 active Cart Horses 3, 5 & 7 years old Property of the Breeder   and a Low locked Phaeton
Dated 27th May, 1856.

W. ROBERTS, PRINTER, 197, HIGH-STREET, EXETER.

328 – Horse sale advert.

329 – The area known as Bonhay, an enclosed open space surrounded by trees was adjacent to The Cattle Market. In 1938 the City Council sold the last of its work horses on the site.

330 – A show of horses on Bonhay.

331 – Horses at the Bonhay site.

332 – Mr Phillips sells horse hames and other agricultural items at the Cattle Market. Circa 1930.

333 – Advert for rams.

Opposite right:

Top: 334 – The Shakespeare Inn on Bonhay Road stood almost opposite the Cattle Market.

Middle: 335 – John Hanson, owner of the Shakespeare Inn.

Bottom: 336 – The Cattle Market Inn, also in Bonhay Road was a natural favourite with local farmers.

Opposite right: 337 – The Star and Garter public house at the corner of Bonhay Road also catered for market traders and farmers.